EARLIER AMERICAN MUSIC
EDITED BY H. WILEY HITCHCOCK
for the *Music Library Association*

2

HORA NOVISSIMA

HORATIO W. PARKER

HORA NOVISSIMA

The Rhythm of Bernard De Morlaix on the Celestial Country
Set to Music for Soli, Chorus, and Orchestra

(Op. 30)

ENGLISH TRANSLATION BY ISABELLA G. PARKER

NEW INTRODUCTION BY H. WILEY HITCHCOCK
Director, Institute for Studies in American Music,
Brooklyn College, CUNY

DA CAPO PRESS • NEW YORK • 1972

This Da Capo Press edition of *Hora Novissima* is an unabridged
republication of the full score originally published in
London and New York in 1900. The program for the service
at which the work was first performed is included herein
as a supplement at the end of the volume.

Library of Congress Catalog Card Number 75-169652
ISBN 0-306-77302-3

Copyright © 1972 by the Music Library Association

Published by Da Capo Press, Inc.
A Subsidiary of Plenum Publishing Corporation
227 West 17th Street, New York, New York 10011

EDITOR'S FOREWORD

American musical culture, from Colonial and Federal Era days on, has been reflected in an astonishing production of printed music of all kinds: by 1820, for instance, more than fifteen thousand musical publications had issued from American presses. Fads, fashions, and tastes have changed so rapidly in our history, however, that comparatively little earlier American music has remained in print. On the other hand, the past few decades have seen an explosion of interest in earlier American culture, including earlier American music. College and university courses in American civilization and American music have proliferated; recording companies have found a surprising response to earlier American composers and their music; a wave of interest in folk and popular music of past eras has opened up byways of musical experience unimagined only a short time ago.

It seems an opportune moment, therefore, to make available for study and enjoyment—and as an aid to furthering performance of earlier American music—works of significance that exist today only in a few scattered copies of publications long out of print, and works that may be well known only in later editions or arrangements having little relationship to the original compositions.

Earlier American Music is planned around several types of musical scores to be reprinted from early editions of the eighteenth, nineteenth, and early twentieth centuries. The categories are as follows:

> Songs and other solo vocal music
> Choral music and part-songs
> Solo keyboard music
> Chamber music
> Orchestral music and concertos
> Dance music and marches for band
> Theater music

The idea of *Earlier American Music* originated in a paper read before the Music Library Association in February, 1968, and published under the title "A Monumenta Americana?" in the Association's journal, *Notes* (September, 1968). It seems most appropriate, therefore, for the Music Library Association to sponsor this series. We hope *Earlier American Music* will stimulate further study and performance of musical Americana.

H. Wiley Hitchcock

INTRODUCTION

Hora Novissima is the most famous American example of the Victorian choral cantata, an American counterpart of Elgar's *Dream of Gerontius* and of a hundred other massive, high-minded choral works written out of the nineteenth-century English passion for community choruses, for musical festivals in which to display them, for oratorios in the tradition of Handel and Mendelssohn for them to sing. America, too, had a long tradition of choral song, going back to the friendly, folkish "singing schools" of the Federal Era and even before. In the nineteenth century, with a change in musical taste toward more elaborate choral-and-orchestral music, rather more formal "musical societies" were established: Boston's Handel and Haydn Society (founded in 1815 and still in existence) was one of the first of this type, Philadelphia's Musical Fund Society (1820–present) another. It was for one of these, the Church Choral Society of New York (J. Pierpont Morgan, President!), that Horatio Parker (1863–1919) composed *Hora Novissima*. The work was first performed by the Society, with organ and special orchestra under Parker's direction, at the Church of the Holy Trinity on May 3, 1893.

Hora Novissima came directly out of Parker's experience, during visits to Britain between 1890 and 1892, of the English choral festivals in such cities as Leeds and Birmingham. However, he also brought to it his solid training in Munich in the 1880's under Josef Rheinberger and his knowledge of works like Dvořák's *Stabat Mater* and the operas and other vocal works of Rossini and Verdi. The result is a composition of undeniable eclecticism—but one integrated by technical devices such as cyclic themes and also by a consistent atmosphere of German-American hymnic grandeur, solidity, and dignity.

The text is from the very long poem, *De Contemptu Mundi,* by a twelfth-century monk of the Abbey of Cluny, Bernard de Morlaix. Parker chose the section describing the glories of heavenly life and voicing a final plea to be allowed to enjoy them. (The English version was the work of Parker's mother.) He divided it into two main parts, with six and five movements respectively, and set it for four soloist, double chorus, organ, and orchestra. The choruses are the pillars of the work; each of the soloists has but a single aria, and the second movement is for the solo quartet.

This spacious work, about an hour in length, is more impressive than entertaining; it is a monument to the ideals of Parker and his fellow-composers of the "Second New England School," according to whose principal spokesman, editor and critic John Sullivan Dwight, music was the language of feeling, its aim to "hallow pleasure, and to naturalize religion."

H.W.H.

HORA NOVISSIMA

COMPOSED FOR THE
CHURCH CHORAL SOCIETY OF NEW YORK.

HORA NOVISSIMA

The Rhythm of Bernard De Morlaix on the Celestial Country

ENGLISH TRANSLATION BY

ISABELLA G. PARKER

SET TO MUSIC FOR SOLI, CHORUS, AND ORCHESTRA

BY

HORATIO W. PARKER.

(OP. 30.)

FULL SCORE.

PRICE TWO GUINEAS.

LONDON: NOVELLO AND COMPANY, LIMITED
AND
NOVELLO, EWER AND CO., NEW YORK.

Copyright, 1900, by Novello and Company, Limited.

TO THE DEAR MEMORY OF MY FATHER

CHARLES EDWARD PARKER

THIS WORK IS GRATEFULLY AND AFFECTIONATELY

DEDICATED.

———————

NEW YORK, DECEMBER, 1892.

CONTENTS.

Hora Novissima.

Introduction and Chorus.— „Hora Novissima."

No 1.

Allegro.

Horatio W. Parker.

Printed by F.M.Geidel, Leipzig.

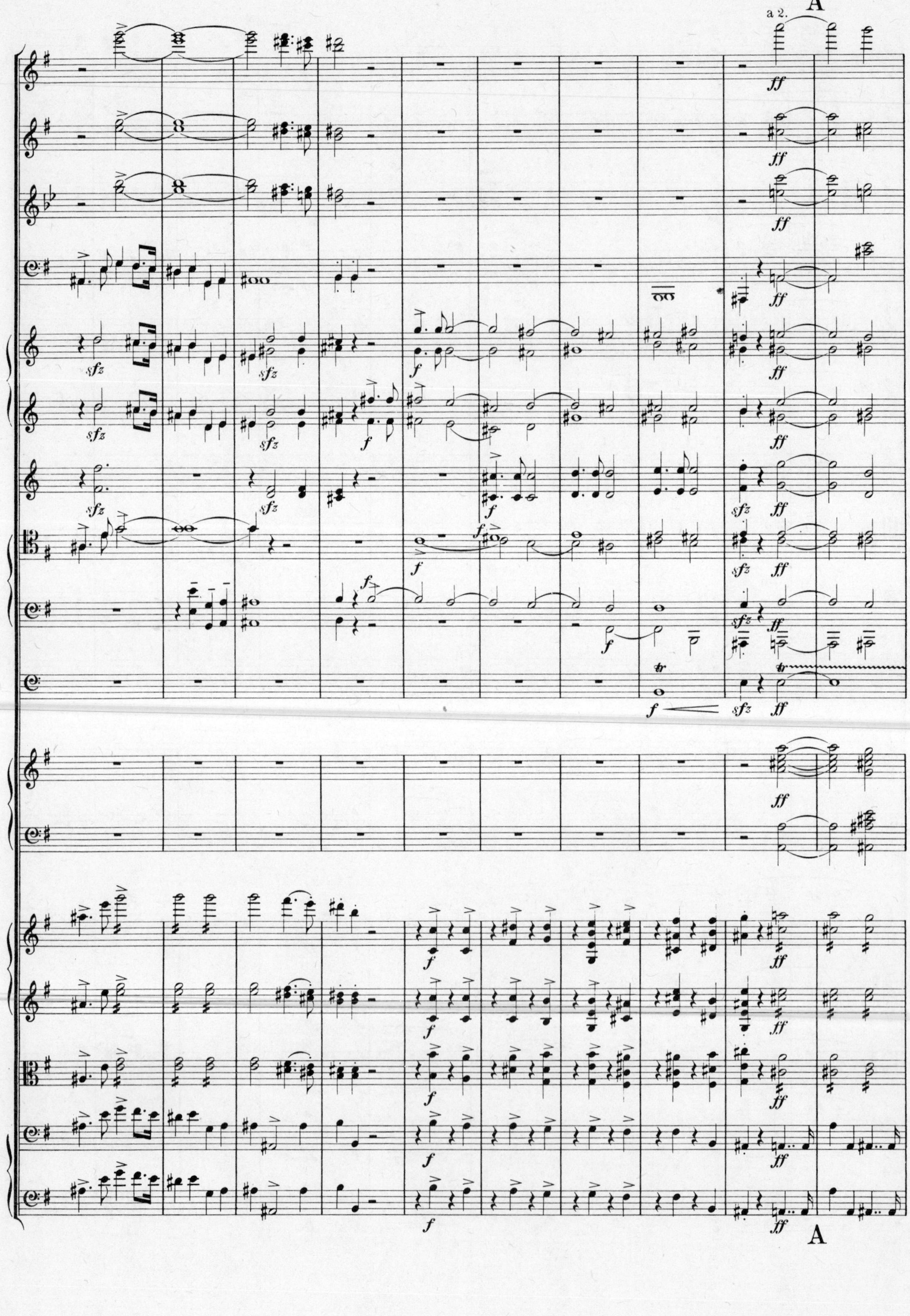
a 2.
A
ff
sfz
f
tr
A

Organo.

im - minet ar - bi-ter, il - le su - pre - -mus.
O'er the un - fold-ing years, Watch-ing for ev - er.
Im-minet, im-minet, et ma-la ter-minet,
Migh-ti-est, migh-ti-est, He is made man-i-fest,

im - minet ar - bi-ter, il - le su - pre - -mus.
O'er the un - fold-ing years, Watch-ing for ev - er.
Im-minet, im-minet, et ma-la ter-minet,
Migh-ti-est, migh-ti-est, He is made man-i-fest,

im - minet ar - bi-ter il - le su - pre -mus.
O'er the un - fold-ing years, Watch-ing for ev - er.
Im-minet, im-minet, et ma-la ter-minet,
Migh-ti-est, migh-ti-est, He is made man-i-fest,

im - minet ar - bi-ter, il - le su - pre - -mus.
O'er the un - fold-ing years, Watch-ing for ev - er.
Im-minet, im-minet, et ma-la ter-minet,
Migh-ti-est, migh-ti-est, He is made man-i-fest,

C

ae - qua cor - o - net.
Right ev - er crowning.

ae - qua cor - o - net.
Right ev - er crowning.

Rec-ta re - mu - ne - ret, anx - i - a li - be-ret,
True hearts in man - sion fair, Free from all anxious care,

ae - qua cor - o - net.
Right ev - er crowning.

ae - qua cor - o - net.
Right ev - er crowning.

Rec-ta re - mu - ne - ret, anx - i - a li - be-ret,
True hearts in man - sion fair, Free from all anxious care,

C

vis- -si-ma, tem- -po- ra pes- -si-ma sunt.
la- -test hour, E- -vil hath migh- -ti-est power.

18

Gr. Cassa e Piatti. *ffz*

tem - po - ra pes - si - ma sunt, vi - gi - -le - mus, vi - gi - -le - -mus!
E - vil hath migh - ti-est power, Keep we vig - il, keep we vig - -il!

tem - po - ra pes-si-ma sunt, vi - gi- -le - mus, vi - gi- -le- -mus!
E - vil hath migh-ti-est power, Keep we vig - il, keep we vig - -il!

tem - po - ra pes-si-ma sunt, vi - gi- -le - mus, vi- -gi-le-mus!
E - vil hath migh - ti-est power, Keep we vig - il, keep we vigil!

tem - po-ra pes - si-ma sunt, vi gi- -le - mus, vi- -gi-le-mus!
E - vil hath migh - ti-est power, Keep we vig - il, keep we vigil!

Gr. Cassa e Piatti

Ped. soft 16 & 8.

32'

div.

div.

div.

div.

vi - gi - le-mus, vi - gi - le - mus.
Keep we vig-il, keep we vig - il.

vi - gi - le-mus, vi - gi - le - mus.
Keep we vig-il, keep we vig - il.

vi - gi - le-mus, vi - gi - le - mus.
Keep we vig-il, keep we vig - il.

vi - gi - le-mus, vi - gi - le - mus.
Keep we vig-il, keep we vig - il.

Quartet. — Hic breve vivitur.

No 2.

Si - de-ra ver-mibus, Op - ti - ma son-tibus, As - tra ma - lig - nis. Sunt mo-dò prae-li-a,
Crowns for the low - li-est, Thrones for the ho - li-est, Heaven's honours shar - ing, Now is the bat - tle hour,

E

Aria (Bass).—"Spe modo vivitur."

No. 3.

ro - - nae;
turn - - ing.

Tunc no - va glo-ri-a pec-to - ra so-bri-a____ cla-ri-fi - ca-bit, cla-ri-fi -
Ev - er new glo-ries still, The in - most heart shall fill,____ With joy su - pernal, with joy su -

ca - bit.
per - nal.
Sol - vet e - nig - ma - ta, Ve - ra - que Sab - ba - ta con - ti - nu - a - bit, con -
All doubts shall dis - appear, When dawneth, calm and clear, Sabbath e - ter - nal, Sab -

ti - nu-a - bit,   nunc   tri-bu - la - ti - o,   tunc re - cre - a - ti - o,   scep-tra, co-ro - nae,   co - ro - nae.
bath   e-ter - nal,   Nox   is the hour of night,   Then, crowned with full delight,   Zi - on re-turn-ing,   re-turn - ing.

pizz.

Chorus. _ "Pars mea, Rex meus."

No 4.

Pars me - a, Rex me-us,
Most Might-y, most Ho-ly,

De-us Ip -se de - co-re, pars me - a, Rex_____ me-us,_____ in pro - pri-o De-us
glo-ry Thy throne en -folding, Most Might - y, most_____ Ho - ly,_____ How great_____ is the glo-ry

Pars me - a, Rex me-us, in pro-pri-o De-us Ip - se de - co-re, pars me - a,
Most Might-y, most Ho-ly, How great is the glo-ry Thy throne en -fold-ing, Most Might - y

Aria. (Soprano). "O Bona Patria."

lu - -mi-na   Col-   - la - cri - man - -tur: Est   tu - a
on___ our ears,   *Sweet*   *be - yond mea - - sure.*   *Thou*   *art the*

78

men - - tio   Pec - - to - ris unc - - tio_____   Cu -
home   of   rest,   And of com - - fort_____   com -

lo - ris, do - lo - - - - - - - - ris.
bro - ken, un - bro - - - - - - - ken.

82

84

Più mosso e molto agitato.

Gr. Cassa e Piatti.

Più mosso e molto agitato.

Più tranquillo.

Rimuta in A.

To - ta ne - go - ti - a, Can - ti - ca dul - ci - a, can - ti - ca dul - ci - a Dul - ce to -
There saints find full em - ploy, Songs of tri - umph-ant joy, songs. of tri - umph - ant joy Ev - er up -

To - ta ne - go - ti - a, Can-ti - ca dul - ci - a, can - ti - ca dul - ci-a Dul - ce to -
There saints find full employ, Songs of tri - umph-ant joy, songs of tri - umph-ant joy Ev - er up -

To - ta ne - go - ti - a, Can-ti - ca dul-ci - a, can - ti - ca dul - ci - a Dul - ce to -
There saints find full employ, Songs of tri - umph-ant joy, songs of tri - umph-ant joy Ev - er up -

To - ta ne - go - ti - a, Can - ti - ca dul-ci - a, can - ti - ca dul - ci - a Dul - ce to -
There saints find full em - ploy, Songs of tri - umph-ant joy, songs of tri - umph - ant joy Ev - er up -

Molto più mosso.

Organo. *fff*

Molto più mosso.

Solo. *fff*

To - ta ne - go - ti - a, ___ con - ju - bi - la - re, ___ con - ju - bi - la - re.
There saints find full em - ploy, *To-gether praising, ___* *to - geth - er prais - ing.*

Sopr.

Alt.

re, to - ta ne - go - ti - a, con - ju - bi - la - re, con - ju - bi - la - re.
ing, *There saints find full employ,* *To-gether praising,* *to - geth - er prais - ing:*

Ten. *fff*

Bass.

Molto più mosso. **End of the first Part.**

Part II.

Aria (Tenor) — Urbs Syon aurea.

№ 7. **Moderato e tranquillo.**

Urbs Sy-on au-re-a, Pa-tri-a lac-te-a, Ci-ve de-co-ra, ci-ve de-co-ra,
Gold-en Je-ru-sa-lem, Bride with her di-a-dem, Ra-diant and glo-rious, ra-diant and glorious,

Om-ne cor ob-ru-is, Om-ni-bus ob-stru-is, Et cor et or-a, cor et
Tem-ple of light thou art, O'er mind, and soul, and heart, Thou art vic-tor-ious, art vic-

E

in om - - ni-a, in - om - - - - - - - ni-a laus tu-a vi -
With heaven - - ly food, with heaven - - - - - - ly food, New life be - stow -

cit.
ing.

Double Chorus. — "Stant Syon atria."

114

119

132

Solo (Alto). "Gens duce splendida."

No 9.

Gens du-ce splendi-da,___ con-ci-o candi-da,___
Peo-ple vic-to-ri-ous,___ *In raiment glori-ous,___*

ves-ti-bus al-bis,___ ves-ti-bus al-bis,___ Sunt si-ne fle-ti-bus
They stand for ev-er,___ they stand for ev-er,___ God wipes a-way their tears,

in Sy - on ae - -di - bus, in Sy - on — ae-di-bus,   ae - -di-bus al - -mis,
Giving, through end - less years, giv - ing, through endless years,   *Peace like a riv - -er.*

138

Sunt si - ne cri - mi - ne, sunt si - ne tur - bi - ne, sunt si - ne li - te In Sy - - on ae - di -
Earth's turmoils end - ed are, Strife and re - proach, and war, No more an - noy - ing, Chil - dren ___ of bless - ed -

bus e - di - ti - o - ri - bus, ___ in ___ Sy - on ae - di - bus, ___
ness, Their he - rit - age of peace, ___ Chil - dren of bless - ed - ness,

cri - mi-ne, si - -ne li - te, si - -ne li - te.
end - ed are, No - -an - noy - ing, no_____ an - noy - ing.

con-ci-o can-di-da,____
*In raiment glo-ri-ous,*____

Sunt si - ne fle-ti-bus____
*God wipes a - way their tears,*____

144

tur - bi - ne,   sunt   si - ne li - te,   si - - ne li - - te. Gens   du - - ce
proach, and war,   *No*   *more an - noy - ing,*   *no   an - noy - - ing. 0*   *peo - - ple*

splen - - - - di-da, splen - - - di-da.
glo - - - - ri-ous, glo - - - ri-ous.

Chorus a Cappella... "Urbs Syon unica."

Nº 10.

Con moto moderato.

Quartet and Chorus._ "Urbs Syon inclyta."

№ 11.

Die kleinen beigefügten Noten sind nur in Ermangelung einer grossen Orgel zu spielen.
The small notes are to be played only when no large organ is available.

C

C

171

Fl.
Ob.
Cl.
Fag.
Arpa.
Organo
pp
Ped. 16
arco
re - us, hac vi - du - a - tus, O
vail - ing, Through Thy own me - rit, O
re - us, hac vi - du - a - tus, O
vail - ing, Through Thy own me - rit, O
re - us, hac vi - du - a - tus,
vail - ing, Through Thy own me - rit,
re - us, hac vi - du - a - tus,
vail - ing, Through Thy own me - rit,
hac vi - du - a - tus, O
Through Thy own me - rit, A
hac vi - du - a - tus, O
Through Thy own me - rit, A
hac vi - du - a - tus, O
Through Thy own me - rit, A
hac vi - du - a - tus, O
Through Thy own me - rit, A
arco
arco

Church Choral Society, New York : : :
Fifth Season : : Eighteen Hundred
and Ninety-two and Ninety-three : :

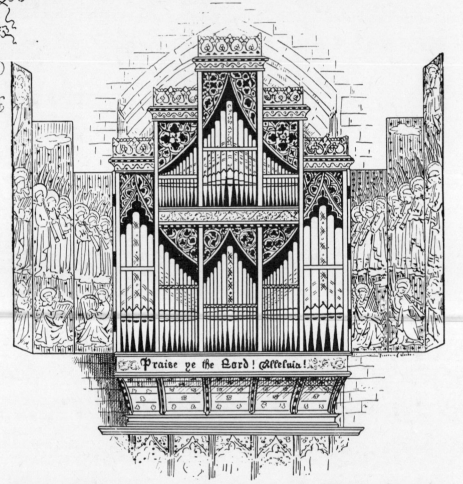

Praise ye the Lord! Alleluia!

Third Service . . Church of the Holy Trinity
Madison Avenue and Forty-second Street . . . . The Rev. E.
Walpole Warren, M. A., Rector : : : : : : : : : : : : : :
Wednesday Evening, May the Third, Eighteen Hundred and
Ninety-three, at half-after Eight o'clock : : : : : : : : : : : :

Mendelssohn, Overture " Athalie " Opus 74.

ORCHESTRA

✠

Service

✠

Apostles' Creed, Lord's Prayer, Collect and Minor Benediction

✠

Hymn 138, " Holy, Holy, Holy."

CONGREGATION, CHOIR, ORGAN AND ORCHESTRA

HOLY, holy, holy ! Lord God Almighty!
Early in the morning our song shall
rise to Thee.
Holy, holy, holy ! merciful and mighty !
God in Three Persons, blessed Trinity.

HOLY, holy, holy ! all the saints adore
Thee,
Casting down their golden crowns
around the glassy sea ;
Cherubim and seraphim falling down be-
fore Thee,
Which wert, and art, and evermore
shalt be.

Holy, holy, holy ! though the darkness
hide Thee,
Though the eye of sinful man Thy glory
may not see,
Only Thou art holy ; there is none beside
Thee
Perfect in power, in love, and purity.

Holy, holy, holy ! LORD GOD Almighty !
All Thy works shall praise Thy Name,
in earth, and sky, and sea :
Holy, holy, holy ! merciful and mighty !
GOD in Three Persons, blessed Trinity!
AMEN.

Horatio W. Parker, - - - - - " Hora Novissima."

First time : Composed for the Society.   Conducted by the composer.

PART I

NO. I.—CHORUS

HORA novissima,
Tempora pessima
Sunt, vigilemus !
Ecce minaciter
Imminet Arbiter
Ille supremus :

Imminet, imminet,
Ut mala terminet,
Æqua coronet,
Recta remuneret,
Anxia liberet,
Æthera donet.

Auferat aspera
Duraque pondera
Mentis onustæ,
Sobria muniat,
Improba puniat,
Utraque juste.

COMETH earth's latest hour,
Evil hath mighty power ;
Now watch we ever—
Keep we vigil.
Lo, the great Judge appears !
O'er the unfolding years :
Watching for ever.

Mightiest, mightiest,
He is made manifest
Right ever crowning —
True hearts in mansion fair,
Free from all anxious care,
Ever enthroning.

Bears He the painful goad,
Lightens the heavy load,
Heavy it must be ;
Giveth the rich reward,
Meteth the penance hard,
Each given justly.

NO. II.—QUARTETTE

HIC breve vivitur,
   Hic breve plangitur,
     Hic breve fletur :
Non breve vivere,
Non breve plangere,
   Retribuetur.

O retributio !
Stat brevis actio,
   Vita perennis ;
O retributio !
Cœlica mansio
   Stat lue plenis ;

Quid datur et quibus
Æther ? egentibus,
   Et cruce dignis,
Sidera vermibus,
Optima sontibus,
   Astra malignis.

Sunt modo prælia,
Postmodo præmia.
   Qualia ? plena :
Plena refectio,
Nullaque passio,
   Nullaque pœna.

HERE life is quickly gone.
   Here grief is ended soon,
     Here tears are flowing ;
Life ever fresh is there,
Life free from anxious care,
   GOD'S hand bestowing.

O blessed Paradise !
Where endless glory lies,
   Rapture unending.
O dwelling full of light,
Where CHRIST'S own presence bright
   Glory is lending.

Who shall this prize attain,
Who this blest guerdon gain,
   Here the cross bearing ?
Crowns for the lowliest,
Thrones for the holiest,
   Heaven's honors sharing.

Now is the battle hour,
Then great rewards our dower.
   What are they ? blessing—
Blessings unknown before,
Passion shall vex no more,
   Peace yet increasing.

NO. III.—ARIA (Bass)

SPE modo vivitur,
   Et Syon angitur
     A Babylone ;
Nunc tribulatio ;
Tunc recreatio,
   Sceptra, coronæ.

Tunc nova gloria
Pectora sobria
   Clarificabit,
Solvet enigmata,
Veraque Sabbata
   Continuabit.

Patria splendida,
Terraque florida,
   Libera spinis,
Danda fidelibus
Est ibi civibus,
   Hic peregrinis.

ZION is captive yet,
   Longing for freedom sweet,
     In exile mourning ;
Now is the hour of night,
Then, crowned with full delight.
   Zion returning.

Ever new glories still
The inmost heart shall fill
   With joy supernal.
All doubts shall disappear,
When dawneth, calm and clear,
   Sabbath eternal.

O country glorious
Love hath prepared for us,
   Thornless thy flowers !
Given to faithful ones,
There to be citizens—
   Such joy be our !

NO. IV.—CHORUS (Introduction and Fugue)

PARS mea, Rex meus,
In proprio Deus
Ipse decore
Visus amabitur,
Atque videbitur
Auctor in ore.

Tunc Jacob Israel,
Et Lia tunc Rachel
Efficietur,
Tunc Syon Atria,
Pulcraque patria
Perficietur.

MOST Mighty, most holy,
How great is the glory
Thy throne enfolding!
When shall we see Thy face,
And all Thy wonders trace,
Joyful beholding?

All the long history,
All the deep mystery,
Through ages hidden.
When shall our souls be blest,
To the great marriage feast
Graciously bidden?

NO. V.—ARIA (Soprano)

O BONA patria,
Lumina sobria
Te speculantur :
Ad tua nomina
Sobria lumina
Collacrymantur :

Est tua mentio
Pectoris unctio,
Cura doloris,
Concipientibus
Æthera mentibus
Ignis amoris.

Tu locus unicus,
Illeque cœlicus
Es paradisus :
Non ibi lacryma,
Sed placidissima
Gaudia, risus.

O COUNTRY bright and fair,
What are thy beauties rare?
What thy rich treasures?
Thy name brings joyful tears,
Falling upon our ears,
Sweet beyond measure.

Thou art the home of rest,
Thy mention to the breast
Gives bliss unspoken.
Who learn thy blessed ways
Shall have, in songs of praise,
Comfort unbroken.

NO. VI.—CHORUS

TU sine littore,
Tu sine tempore,
Fons, modo rivus,
Dulce bonis sapis,
Estque tibi lapis
Undique vivus.

Est tibi laurea,
Dos datur aurea,
Sponsa decora,
Primaque Principis
Oscula suscipis,
Inspicis ora.

Candida lilia,
Vivia monilia,
Sunt tibi, sponsa,
Agnus adest tibi,
Sponsus adest tibi,
Lux speciosa.

THOU ocean without shore,
Where time shall be no more,
Dwelling most gracious.
Fountain of love alone,
Thou hast the living stone,
Elect and precious.

Thou hast the laurel fair,
The heavenly Bride shall wear,
Robed in her splendor.
First shall the Prince confer
All priceless gifts on her,
With glances tender.

There are the lilies white,
In garlands pure and bright,
Her brow adorning.
The Lamb her Spouse shall be,
His light shines gloriously,
Fairer than morning.

Tota negotia,
Cantica dulcia
  Dulce tonare,
Tam mala debita,
Quam bona præbita,
  Conjubilare.

There saints find full employ,
Songs of triumphant joy
  Ever upraising.
They who are most beloved,
They who where tried and pro
  Together praising.

✠

PART II

NO. VII.—ARIA (Tenor)

URBS Syon aurea,
  Patria lactea,
    Cive decora,
Omne cor obruis,
Omnibus obstruis
  Et cor et ora,

Nescio, nescio,
Quæ jubilatio,
  Lux tibi qualis,
Quam socialia
Gaudia, gloria
  Quam specialis:

Laude studens ea
Tollere, mens mea
  Victa fatiscit;
O bona gloria,
Vincor; in omnia
  Laus tua vicit.

GOLDEN Jerusalem,
  Bride with her diadem,
    Radiant and glorious;
Temple of light thou art,
O'er mind and soul and heart,
  Thou art victorious.

Who can tell—who can tell
  What noble anthems swell
  Through thy bright portal?
What dear delights are thine,
What glory most divine,
  What light immortal!

Longing thy joys to sing,
Worthily offering
  Love overflowing;
Glory most bright and good,
Feed me with heavenly food,
  New life bestowing.

NO. VIII.—DOUBLE CHORUS

STANT Syon atria
  Conjubilantia,
    Martyre plena
Cive micantia,
Principe stantia,
  Luce serena;

Est ibi pascua
Mitibus afflua,
  Praestita sanctis;
Regis ibi thronus,
Agminis et sonus
  Est epulantis.

THERE stand those halls on high,
  There sound the songs of joy
    In noblest measure.
There are the martyrs bright
In heaven's o'erflowing light—
  The LORD's own treasure,

In pastures fresh and green
The white-robed saints are seen,
  For ever resting;
The kingly throne is near,
And joyful shouts we hear,
  Of many feasting.

NO. IX.—ARIA (Alto)

GENS duce splendida,
  Concio candida,
    Vestibus albis,
Sunt sine fletibus
In Syon ædibus,
  Ædibus almis;

Sunt sine crimine,
Sunt sine turbine,
  Sunt sine lite
In Syon ædibus
Editioribus
  Israelitæ

PEOPLE victorious,
  In raiment glorious,
    They stand forever.
God wipes away their tears,
Giving, through endless years,
  Peace like a river.

Earth's turmoils ended are,
Strife, and reproach, and war,
  No more annoying:
Children of blessedness
Their heritage of peace
  Freely enjoying.

URBS Syon unica,
  Mansio mystica,
    Condita cœlo,
Nunc tibi gaudeo,
Nunc mihi lugeo,
  Tristor, anhelo ;

Te quia corpore
Non queo, pectore
  Sæpe penetro ;
Sed, caro terrea,
Terraque carnea,
  Mox cado retro.

CITY of high renown,
  Home of the saints alone,
    Built in the heaven ;
Now will I sing thy praise,
Adore the matchless grace
  To mortals given.

Vainly I strive to tell
All thy rich glories well,
  Thy beauty singing ;
Still, with the earnest heart,
Bear I my humble part,
  My tribute bringing.

NO. XI.—QUARTETTE AND CHORUS

Out of respect to Members of the Congregation who wish to hear the
Service undisturbed to its conclusion, a pause will be made before the
final number, when those who are unable to remain to the end are
courteously requested to retire.

URBS Syon inclyta,
  Turris et edita
    Littore tuto,
Te Peto, te colo,
Te flagro, te volo,
  Canto, saluto ;

Nec meritis peto ;
Nam meritis meto
  Morte perire ;
Nec reticens tego,
Quod meritis ego
  Filius iræ.

Vita quidem mea,
Vita nimis rea,
  Mortua vita
Quippe reatibus
Exitialibus
  Obruta, trita.

Spe tamen ambulo,
Præmia postulo
  Speque fideque ;
Illa perennia
Postulo præmia
  Nocte dieque.

Me Pater optimus
Atque piissimus
  Ille creavit,
In lue pertulit,
Ex lue sustulit,
  A lue lavit.

THOU city great and high,
  Towering beyond the sky,
    Storms reach thee never :
I seek thee, long for thee ;
I love thee, I sing thee,
  I hail thee ever.

Though I am unworthy
Of mercy before Thee,
  Justly I perish ;
My follies confessing,
Nor claiming Thy blessing,
  No hope I cherish.

In deepest contrition,
Owning my condition,
  My life unholy ;
Burdened with guiltiness,
Weary and comfortless,
  Help, I implore Thee.

Yet will I faithfully
Strive those rewards to see,
  Beck'ning so brightly ;
Ask in unworthiness
Heavenly blessedness,
  Daily and nightly.

For He, the Father blest,
Wisest and holiest,
  Of life the Giver,
Maketh His light to shine
In this dark soul of mine,
  Dwelling for ever.

O bona patria,	O land of full delight,
Num tua gaudia	Thy peerless treasures bright,
Teque videbo?	May we behold them !
O bona patria,	Thou home of beauty rare,
Num tua præmia	May we thy blessings share !
Plena tenebo?	Priceless we hold them,
O sacer, O pius,	O blessed for ever
O ter et amplius	A thousandfold they are
Ille beatus,	That rest attaining,
Cui sua pars Deus ;	Most blessed and holy
O miser, O reus,	With Thee in Thy glory
Hac viduatus.	For ever reigning.

COLLECT AND BENEDICTION

Soloists

MRS. THEODORE J. TOEDT, Soprano

MISS RUTH THOMPSON, Contralto

MR. S. FISCHER MILLER, Tenore

MR. ERICKSSON BUSHNELL, Bass

MR. WILL C. MACFARLANE, Organist

✤

Chorus

THE ACTIVE MEMBERS OF THE CHURCH CHORAL SOCIETY

✤

Orchestra and Organ

Church Choral Society, New York, Season of Eighteen Hundred and Ninety-two and Ninety-three : : : : : : : : :

✠

Officers

PRESIDENT
J. PIERPONT MORGAN

FIRST VICE-PRESIDENT
THE RT. REVD. H. C. POTTER, D.D., LL.D.

SECOND-VICE PRESIDENT
THE REVD. DAVID H. GREER, D.D.

SECRETARY AND TREASURER   ASSISTANT TREASURER
HENRY LEWIS MORRIS   J. MIDAUGH MAIN
16 EXCHANGE PLACE   666 FIFTH AVENUE

MUSICAL DIRECTOR
RICHARD HENRY WARREN
344 MADISON AVENUE

✠

Board of Governors

Rt. Revd. H. C. Potter, D.D., LL.D.   Daniel T. Hoag
Rev. John W. Brown, D.D.   John Murray Mitchell
  "   David H. Greer, D.D.   J. Pierpont Morgan
  "   D. Parker Morgan, D.D.   Henry Lewis Morris
  "   William S. Rainsford, D.D.   Gordon Norrie
  "   Henry Y. Satterlee, D.D.   George Foster Peabody
  "   E. Walpole Warren, M.A.   Gustave Schwab
George A. Crocker   Anson Phelps Stokes
Arthur B. Graves   Frederick D. Tappen
James G. Goodwin   George W. Vanderbilt
Joseph W. Harper   Richard Henry Warren
Henry W. Hayden   John H. Watson